Loons

Loons

ROBERT H. BUSCH

Whitecap Books

Vancouver / Toronto / New York

Edited by Elaine Jones
Scientific review by Ted Gostomski
Proofread by Elizabeth McLean
Cover design by Steve Penner
Interior design by Margaret Ng
Desktop publishing by Jennifer Conroy
Cover photograph by Tim Christie

Printed in Canada.

Canadian Cataloguing in Publication Data

Busch, Robert H., 1953–
    Loons

    Copublished by Prospero.
    Includes index.
    ISBN 1-55110-928-X (Whitecap)—ISBN 1-894102-44-4

    1. Loons. 2. Loons—Pictorial works. I. Title.
QL696.G33B87 1999   598.4'42   C99-910260-5

Some birds represent the majesty of nature, like the eagles;
others its sweetness and melody, like song birds.
The small loon represents its wildness and solitariness.

—John Burroughs, *Leaf & Tendril*

CONTENTS

INTRODUCTION

MAGIC IN THE WILDERNESS

I t's just a piddly little pond, a pockmark on the face of the forest. Pale-skinned aspens line one bank, white wildflowers at their feet. Dragonflies thrash and rustle in the reeds, and black-and-brown salamanders roam the pond's edge, in coats so glossy they appear freshly varnished. After the last gasp of winter, the pond is a siren for the senses: a blackwater creek gurgles into one side of it, the sharp scent of pines wafts across it, and in the middle of it, a pair of boldly checkered loons bob on top of the sun-slashed water.

I have spent many hours watching those loons, admiring their striking plumage and glowing inside whenever their unearthly calls pierce the cool still air.

Like many others, I am in love with loons.

My most memorable experience with loons came late one summer afternoon. As the air chilled and dusk blushed the sky to pastel tones of peach and pink, two loons appeared

PREVIOUS PAGE, LEFT: *Both loons and grebes perform an aquatic "penguin dance" to scare off intruders. The dance is one of the most fascinating facets of loon behavior, but it always denotes stress or fear and is a clear sign to human observers to retreat.*

PREVIOUS PAGE, RIGHT: *According to an Algonquin legend, Kuloskap, one of the most senior of gods, was hunting on a lakeshore one day when he saw a loon flying above him. Kuloskap asked the loon if they could be friends and the loon agreed. Kuloskap then taught the loon its special laughing cry so that the loon could act as his messenger. The loon thus became a go-between between the gods and the Algonquin people, and was treated with great respect.*

on the far side of the pond. They swam long lazy loops around one bay, heads submerged as they searched for supper. Suddenly a lone grebe paddled out of the rushes, its angular head distinctive even from my distant hidey-hole. The loons took one look at the intruder and attacked immediately, splashing noisily toward it in a show of bravado that sent the bashful bird skyward in search of more friendly waters.

One of the loons called after it, dropping its lower bill and rapidly clapping it up again to create the eery "laugh" for which the bird is so famous: *oo-oo-OO-OO-OO-oo-oo.*

A few minutes later, an answering call arose from the woods across the pond: a

LEFT: *This Thayer's gull is harassing a Pacific loon; although the two species are close relations, they seldom tolerate each other's presence on the same body of water. Gulls are also significant predators of loon chicks.*

wavering chorus of wolf howls. And for some time the two species—two powerful symbols of
the North—sang a wilderness duet that echoed back and forth in the still evening air.

It was the wildest sound I have ever heard.

Those loons at that remote wilderness pond were common loons, a bland name for so striking a bird.

The loon family first evolved about 70 million years ago in northern Europe. The modern
loon appeared on the scene some 60 million years later. It is thought that walls of ice during
the last ice age cut off loon populations and led to the evolution of five separate species, four
of which are commonly found in North America. All adult loons are duck-sized, with pointed
bills, red eyes, small wings, and large webbed feet.

Best known is the common loon (*Gavia immer*), also known as the great speckled diver
and the great northern diver. From the tip of the bill to the tip of the tail, common loons measure 65 to 90 centimetres (about 25 to 35 inches). They weigh 2 to 7 kilograms (about 4 to
14 pounds).

Common loons are the flamboyant divas of the loon family. Adults in breeding plumage
have a beautiful velvety black head with ruby-red eyes and a daggerlike black bill. If you get
close enough, you may see a faint greenish-purple sheen on the head feathers, like the rain-
bow of colors at the edges of soap bubbles. The common loon's neck is black with two flashy
decorations. At the front of the throat is a half necklace of a dozen small white dots. Beneath
this is a larger white-striped collar that wraps around the back of the neck, as if two fingers
dipped in white paint had grabbed the neck from behind. The collar patterns vary from bird

to bird, and can sometimes be used to distinguish individuals.

The chest of the common loon is white with radiating stripes that flow into the back. The black and white back is stark and striking, a complex pattern of squarish white splotches and small white dots on a background of the deepest black. Although the checkered back seems showy to some eyes, it actually is excellent camouflage against sunlight-dappled choppy water. The stomach of the bird is pure white, providing good camouflage from below. Males and females share the same plumage.

The Arctic loon (*Gavia arctica*), or black-throated diver, is a smaller cousin of the common loon and is primarily resident in Eurasia, although it does nest in western Alaska. It is 65 to 75 centimetres long (about 25 to 30 inches) and weighs 1.5 to 3 kilograms (about 3 to 7 pounds). The head of the Arctic loon is charcoal gray. It has a black throat patch with fine white vertical lines; in the right light the patch shows a gorgeous dark green sheen.

The Pacific loon (*Gavia pacifica*), or Pacific diver, was not recognized as a separate species from the Arctic loon until 1985. Both species are the same length and weight. The Pacific loon has a lighter gray head than the Arctic loon, with a metallic purplish sheen to its throat patch. Both Pacific and Arctic loons have four large patches of white splotches on their backs.

The yellow-billed loon (*Gavia adamsii*) is the largest member of the loon family and the one that most resembles the common loon. It is 75 to 100 centimetres long (about 30 to 40 inches) and weighs 4.5 to 7 kilograms (about 10 to 15 pounds). The yellow-billed loon can be distinguished by a large yellow bill that is upturned, giving it a slightly snobbish appearance. It also has a distinctive bump on its forehead.

The red-throated loon (*Gavia stellata*), or red-throated diver, is the runt of the loon family. It is 65 centimetres (about 25 inches) long and weighs 1 to 2 kilograms (about 2 to 4 pounds). The red-throated loon has an olive-gray head with fine white lines and a throat patch the color of newly minted pennies. Its back lacks the flashy upholstery of its cousins, with only a few white spots on a mottled gray background.

No bird except the eagle is the star of so many legends and folk tales, and many of these relate to the loon's striking coloration.

One tale told by the Inuit of Alaska explains the necklace of white that graces common and yellow-billed loons. Long ago, a blind boy lived along the ocean, spending his lonely days threading seashells onto a necklace. One day his mean grandmother told him to go out and be useful, ordering him to catch a loon for supper. The boy did as he was told and successfully snared a loon. But as he picked it up, the loon spoke to him, begging for its life and promising to restore the boy's sight if he dove into the water. The boy climbed on the loon's back and repeatedly dove into the frigid northern waters until his sight miraculously returned. In thanks, the boy gave the loon his necklace made of shells, hanging it around the bird's neck, where it is visible even today.

Another story relates to the loon's black and white coat. According to the Greenland Inuit, long ago all birds were white. When it came time for them to receive their colors, Loon and Raven agreed to paint each other. Raven painted Loon first, using blackened ashes to coat the

bird. Then Raven used his bill to dab white over the black, to echo the stars of the night. When it was Loon's turn, he began to paint Raven in a similar coat of black, but Raven became impatient, telling Loon to hurry. Loon finally gave up and just threw ashes all over Raven. And that is why the raven today is all black but the loon is black and white.

Loons may be dressed for success, but unless they maintain their feathers, they lose both waterproofing and buoyancy. Loons preen by squeezing oil from a gland at the base of the tail onto their bills and then drawing feathers through their bills to oil them. Five to seven minutes per hour may be spent preening. The oil provides excellent waterproofing for swimming, and indeed most of the loon's day is spent cruising serenely around its pond looking for food. Loons often swim with their heads underwater, searching for fish.

Loons eat a wide variety of small fish, with occasional snacks of insects, amphibians, and vegetation. One loon was even observed picking up a large mussel and gulping it down shell and all. Contrary to some folk tales, loons do not spear fish with their pointed bills. Instead, they grab them with an open beak. Small fish are usually eaten underwater; larger fish are most often brought to the surface.

In order to pursue their prey, loons are capable of deep dives, sometimes reaching depths of 33 metres (108 feet). There is even one anecdotal report of a loon entangled in fishing lines at a depth of 73 metres (240 feet). Unlike most birds, loons have heavy marrow-filled bones, permitting them to sink rapidly. They are able to store large amounts of oxygen dissolved in the blood of the muscles, allowing them to stay

PREVIOUS PAGE: *According to a Micmac legend, loons were once land birds, but could not walk well. When Loon was invited to a feast, his awkward gait embarrassed the host, who grabbed Loon and threatened him. Loon cleverly begged for any punishment except being thrown in the water. The host promptly threw Loon into the water, and the lucky bird swam away, seldom to return to land.*

RIGHT: *The yellow-billed loon is the largest loon species. Its greatest numbers in North America are probably in the National Petroleum Reserve Alaska, where its habitat is threatened by oil exploration.*

submerged for up to 15 minutes. Most dives, however, last less than a minute. Underwater, loons propel themselves with their large webbed feet, with the wings held tightly closed. They rarely use their wings to swim underwater, employing them only to turn or to hit the brakes.

The combination of heavy bones and short wings makes it difficult for loons to become airborne. Common loons may require over a third of a kilometre (a quarter-mile) of water from which to take off if there is no wind to assist them. Once in the air, loons are excellent fliers, easily zipping along at 98 kilometres (61 miles) an hour and capable of hitting 135 kilometres (84 miles) an hour over a short stretch.

On land, however, the loon is at a distinct disadvantage. Its legs are located far back on its body, perfect for swimming, but making walking very awkward. In fact, the word "loon" may come from the old Scandinavian term *løm,* meaning a clumsy person.

A number of legends account for the awkward position of the loon's legs. The Anishinabeg natives of the American woodlands used to tell the story of their folk hero Naneboujou, who once chased a loon in anger and kicked it, pushing its legs far back of their normal position, where they have stayed to this day. According to a Finnish legend, Mother Nature originally made the loon without legs, but when she realized her mistake, she quickly stuck on a pair, not looking exactly where they were supposed to go.

Loons are highly territorial and actively chase off other birds—particularly other loons. This aggression is suspended when food is abundant and during the migration period. In a 1795 book, explorer Samuel Hearne incorrectly wrote that you only find one pair of loons per lake, saying this was "a great proof of their aversion to society." In fact, larger lakes often support a number of loon pairs, each defending a favorite bay against invaders.

Usually threat displays are all that is necessary, in which a loon swims rapidly toward another bird, splashing frantically. Sometimes a loon may rear up off the water to run toward an intruder in what's been called a "penguin dance," achieving speeds up to 24 kilometres (15 miles) an hour.

Loons even swim below other birds and stab them from beneath with their strong bills. There is one record of a loon killing an adult Canada goose in such a sneak underwater attack. Male loons can be especially aggressive. One overeager nature photographer in Minnesota was stabbed in the face by the beak of an irate male loon and now knows why the Ojibwa word for loon is *mahng,* which also means brave.

While defending their territory, male loons often emit a long yodeling sound that is only a small part of their vocal repertoire. Biologists who have studied loon calls divide them into four categories: wails, tremolos, yodels, and hoots.

The wail is a short warble that is used to bring loons closer to each other, the loon equivalent of "I am here. Where the heck are you?" It is also used to call chicks off a nest, or to lure a mate to come closer. The tremolo, or bubbly laugh, denotes fear or excitement, often used when danger appears. If the source of danger is you, it's a clear signal to back off. The yodel is used by males to warn other birds of their trespassing or to state territorial rights.

PREVIOUS PAGE: *Like many other aquatic species, loons generally have dark backs, with lighter colors under the wings and on the breast and stomach. This two-tone coloring provides excellent protection from predators both above and below the water's surface.*

RIGHT: *In deep water, red appears black, so the bright red eye of the loon is probably not visible to fish. All a fish likely sees is yet another black shadow among many in the murky depths — until it's too late.*

Hoots are short contact calls, used by loons in close proximity or by parents communicating to hatching chicks or chicks about to enter the water.

Wails, tremolos, yodels, and hoots — four words that describe the sounds of the loon, but none of the soul. Together, the four calls add an air of magic to the often silent world of the wild. Together, they are the sound of the North.

RIGHT: *Many loon nests are located right at the water's edge for reasons of security. A loon's legs are located far back on its body, making it a clumsy walker. In fact, the word loon may originate from the old Scandinavian term* løm, *meaning a clumsy person, which is the same root word for the English term lummox. Alternatively, it may derive from the Old Icelandic* lomr, *meaning awkward.*

LEFT AND ABOVE: *Loons often swim with their heads submerged, looking for fish, which they pursue with a smooth rolling dive. The French word for loon,* plongeon, *actually means diver. The common loon's Latin name,* Gavia immer, *means diving gull.*

RIGHT: *Using their powerful leg muscles, loons can rear up above the water and run toward intruders at speeds of up to 24 kilometres per hour (15 miles per hour).*

ABOVE: *This rare shot of a loon swimming underwater shows its streamlined form, with head outstretched and wings tightly folded. The large webbed feet are used for propulsion, pushing loons to depths of 33 metres (108 feet) or more. During a deep dive, the loon's heart rate may decrease by about half, to slow the use of oxygen.*

RIGHT: *The loon's strong webbed feet propel it forcefully through the water. Their placement to the rear of the body has led to one of the bird's less flattering nicknames—arsefoot.*

LEFT: *There are an estimated 20 000 common loons in the lower 48 states. About 15 000 are found in Minnesota and Wisconsin.*

FAR LEFT: *This photo shows a Pacific loon, which was not recognized as a separate species from the Arctic loon by the American Ornithologists Union until 1985. Biologists in the U.S.S.R. had separated the two many years earlier, but it took a relaxation of Communist publication restrictions to make their research available to westerners.*

ABOVE: *In 1763, Danish naturalist Erik Pontoppidan thought he saw a bright red star in the red-throated loon's copper-colored throat patch, so he named the bird* Gavia stellata, *which means "starry gull."*

RIGHT: *The flamboyant common loon is the best-known loon in North America. At one time, the nesting range of the common loon stretched as far south as Pennsylvania. Today, the bird is rare south of Massachusetts.*

RIGHT: *The Inuit of Canada's North call the loon* tuu'lik. *It means having a dagger or tusk, and refers to the stout bill. Contrary to some folk tales, loons do not spear fish, but grab them, scissorlike, with open bills.*

ON THE WATERFRONT

LIVING LIKE A LOON

Early one morning, I watched wisps of mist swirl above the water of my little pond, transforming it into a place of mystery. Suddenly, two loons materialized, seemingly from nowhere. For the next half-hour, they entranced me with their dances and dives of passion, for there are few sights in nature more striking than that of loons in love.

In a typical courtship between common loons, an eager male will swim toward a female, regularly dipping his head underwater. To human onlookers, it looks as if he is bowing to her. He may almost touch heads with his intended mate before suddenly diving beneath her. She, in turn, may indicate her interest by diving beneath him. The two may then flap their wings vigorously, snapping their feathers back in place after submersion. After they're too pooped to paddle, the loony lovers may swim sedately around each

PREVIOUS PAGE, LEFT: *These loons are resting on Wonder Lake in spectacular Denali National Park, Alaska. Although the common loon is doing well in Alaska, the red-throated loon has shown sharp declines, for reasons unknown.*

PREVIOUS PAGE, RIGHT: *Incubating loons often stand and reposition themselves every hour or so, adding bits of vegetation until the nest is more comfortable. After three or four hours on the nest, a loon may call for its partner to relieve it.*

other in circles or swim side by side like two seniors out for a stroll. The total bonding period may stretch out over two or three weeks.

Other loon species are just as romantic. One ornithologist in Europe studied the courtship of red-throated loons and described a posture in which the back half of the loons' bodies submerges underwater so that the front half is raised up at a 45-degree angle, bills pointing skyward. The two birds thus look like ancient plesiosaurs, or like the famous grainy photo that is supposed to be the head and neck of the Loch Ness monster. The pair then dip their bills into the water, dive past each other, and swim tightly in formation, one behind the other, in a classic exhibition of synchronized swimming.

LEFT: *Loons have been called "feathered fish" due to their aquatic lifestyle. According to some studies, 99 percent of the common loon's time, outside of the nesting stage, is spent on or in the water.*

If all goes well, the courtship results in copulation. This usually takes place on land, near the water's edge, with the male loon mounting the female from the rear for a quick 5- to 10-second breeding. Although people once believed that loons mate for life, a recent study on Lake Superior found that one-fifth of the loons studied there switched mates or territories each spring upon arrival at the breeding ponds.

Each loon species prefers a different size of breeding pond, nature's way of spreading the species around to prevent interbreeding. (There is, however, one record of a common loon/ yellow-billed loon hybrid from Ontario and a few records of common loon/Arctic loon hybrids from Scotland.) Loons will also nest alongside the ocean on occasion.

Pacific and Arctic loons prefer to nest along large bodies of water. The Pacific loon nests across most of Alaska and northern Canada west of Hudson Bay. Its near twin the Arctic loon nests along northern Eurasia, from Norway east to the Kamchatka Peninsula of the Russian Federation and western Alaska.

Common loons prefer larger ponds that are usually at least 25 hectares (10 acres). They breed throughout a band that stretches from Alaska right across most of Canada and dips into the northeastern United States.

Red-throated loons often nest at the edges of small ponds, and can take flight from tiny bodies of water that would strand their bigger cousins. They are the only loon that can take off from land. Red-throated loons are one of the most northerly breeding birds in the world, sometimes nesting just 800 kilometres (500 miles) from the North Pole. They can be found from the Aleutian Islands east along the northern rim of North America, in many of the

LEFT: *Courting loons may vigorously shake their wings, making the water dance with their passion. They may also swim toward each other with bills pointed skyward, heads turning coyly from side to side.*

Arctic islands, and along the coast of Greenland. Yellow-billed loons nest primarily on large lakes in the central Arctic of North America and east to Eurasia.

The placement of their legs far back on the body makes walking difficult, so most loons nest very close to the water's edge. Common loons show a distinct preference for nesting on islands. There are three records from British Columbia of common loons actually making their own floating islands out of reeds and grasses.

Loon nests are constructed by both partners soon after copulation. With Arctic loons, the male actually does most of the initial work. The nests may be simple scrapes in the ground or large mounds 60 centimetres (24 inches) in diameter and 45 centimetres (18 inches) high, depending on how ambitious the loons are and the nesting material that is available. One loon in northern Alberta made no nest at all, laying her eggs in a hollow on top of a pond-side boulder. More typically, small sticks and bottom vegetation are used to build a low nest with a saucer-shaped depression in the middle. The nests are not feathered. Loons seem to feel very secure in these waterside constructions, sitting tight until the last possible moment if danger appears.

A few days after copulation occurs, the female lays two, and occasionally three, large olive-brown oval eggs in the nest. In North America, most loon eggs are laid by May. During the laying process, the female pants and rolls her body from side to side, occasionally raising and lowering her tail. She may spend hours laying one egg and often waits a day before laying her second egg.

The male and female loon take turns incubating the eggs, often for stints of about four

PREVIOUS PAGE: *This loon has chosen a beautiful patch of flowery vegetation for its nest site. The northern edge of the nesting range for the common loon approximates the tree line across northern Alaska and Canada.*

hours each. The birds turn the precious eggs with their bills about once an hour.

If an enemy appears, the nest-sitter squats low on the nest, with its neck outstretched. This decreases the profile of the bird and covers up the bright white chest. The mate that is not on the nest will attempt to scare off predators by swimming rapidly toward them and splashing water.

So strong is the instinct to defend the nest that loons continue to defend their empty nests long after chicks have grown and gone. Males defend their nests and territories more aggressively than they defend their mates. Nests are often reused from one year to the next, in one of nature's many examples of recycling. One nest in British Columbia was used for four years in a row.

LEFT: *This red-throated loon is turning its eggs, which it does about once an hour. Incubating loons always sit facing the water, laying their heads on the edge of the nest to avoid detection in what has been termed a crouch posture. The slightest sound results in a graceful slide into the water, followed by calls of alarm.*

After about 29 days, a faint peeping can be heard from inside the eggs. The nestlings use a sharp point on the upper surface of their beaks, called the egg tooth, to break through the shell and emerge into the big wild world. Their struggle may take an hour or so, or even half a day. The egg tooth drops off after a day or two. The mother loon eats the smallest bits of shell and discards the rest into the water.

At this point in their lives, loon chicks are little more than fluff and appetite. They grow quickly on tiny fish and insects offered by the parents, but sometimes the parents get too ambitious and attempt to stuff overly large fish into their little chicks. It is not unusual to see a chick with the rear half of a fish sticking out of its beak for an hour or two until the front half is finally swallowed.

As the chicks grow, their parents begin to tempt them with live food, dropping injured minnows in front of them to bring out the hunting instinct. Usually the larger of the two chicks gets the lion's share of the food. The smallest chick often starves or is killed by its sibling. Chicks learn to catch their own fish by the age of about two months.

Loon chicks may take to the water within hours of hatching. They have an instinctive attraction to water, swimming behind either parent and hopping onto its back for a free ride, a move which always elicits a chorus of *ahhhhhs* from human onlookers. Chicks will also hide under a parent's wing, leading many early peoples to believe that loon chicks hatch through holes under the mother's wings.

Chicks are eager divers, but their thick coat of down traps a lot of air, making them pop right back up again like corks. A young loon's first molt takes place after about four weeks, changing its initial coat of charcoal gray to a henna-red color. At five or six weeks, the loons

LEFT: *During the days just prior to the hatching of loon eggs, the tiny chicks peep feebly, causing great excitement among the parents. The chicks may take half a day to hatch. They emerge soaking wet, taking several hours to dry into cute little balls of fluff.*

molt again to a mottled gray color. The full dazzling adult plumage doesn't develop until the birds are about two or three years old, when they also reach sexual maturity.

As their flight feathers develop, young loons increasingly paddle like mad across their ponds, using their tiny wings as oars. They flap harder and harder until that magical day when, probably to their total surprise, they actually lift off in their first short flight. This can occur anywhere from 11 to 13 weeks after birth.

A long list of predators likes nothing better than a nice loon lunch. Young chicks in particular are gobbled up by gulls, eagles, mink, skunks, foxes, northern pike, muskellunge, snapping turtles, and raccoons. In some areas, only one loon chick in sixteen survives the first three months of life.

By late summer, adult loons gather prior to migration into groups ranging from a few birds to a few hundred. The parent birds are the first to head south, usually in September or October, leaving their young behind. Loons may migrate singly, in pairs, or in large accumulations of hundreds of irregularly spaced individuals. After a few quick days of flying practice, the juveniles also head south for the winter, while human observers remain in the north and shiver until spring.

Consider for a minute the miracle of migration for a young loon: It has never before seen ice, has probably never left its natal pond, and yet some instinct guides it away from the only home it has ever known to wintering grounds it has never seen before. We still don't know just how they do it.

In North America, most loons winter in California, Baja California, and Florida. In Asia, the Arctic loon winters as far south as central China. Depending on where they

summer, loons may migrate a short distance or over 1600 kilometres (a thousand miles), flying by day and resting at night. They arrive at the wintering grounds anywhere from September through November. Large numbers of loons may migrate past one point during these months; on November 15, 1958, a record 17 000 Pacific loons were counted passing Point Pinos, California.

Once at the wintering grounds, loons exchange their classy checkered plumage for drab brown and gray coats that look like thrift store rejects. In fact, wintering loons were classed as a separate species until biologists realized their mistake. The molt may take from a week to a month, during which time the flightless birds are highly susceptible to predators. The birds tend to stay far out at sea, however, and move at night to deeper water to avoid the numerous coastal dangers. Around January, the loons again change into their striking breeding plumage. They thus undergo only one complete molt per year, unlike most other birds, which molt twice a year. Only the red-throated loon follows the normal avian pattern.

In March or April, some inner sense tells loons to hit the road once again and they fly back north to the breeding lakes. The males usually arrive first to stake out territories, landing after their long flights with a clumsy belly flop that makes for a very splashy entrance. Sometimes the birds crash-land on blacktopped highways, which from high above look just like long stretches of water.

Loons that avoid the rivers of asphalt may live to the age of 25 or even 30 years. The Inuit of Canada's North were well aware of the birds' longevity and once wiped newborn babies with loon skins to assure them of a long life. However, many loons die in their first year of life, unable to avoid the biggest predator of them all: humankind.

PREVIOUS PAGE: *Adult loons initially feed their young by holding food out to them, requiring the chicks to reach and grab. They then drop live food in front of the chicks, teaching them to pursue it. These early lessons often end in failure, with the patient parents diving to retrieve dropped food and trying again and again until the chicks succeed.*

LEFT: *A loon chick often rests by catching a ride on its parent's back. This common loon chick is getting a bit big for hitch-hiking. The bond between a chick and its parents is formed as soon as the chick hatches and imprints on the parents' striking coloration.*

LEFT: *A pair of red-throated loons and their chicks. Despite the ferocity with which loons defend their young, the parents abandon the chicks in the fall and migrate south without them. After a little more flying practice, the young loons follow. Chicks that have not learned to fly by then are doomed to die from starvation or predation. Arctic and red-throated loon chicks often are stranded when they wait too long and their northern ponds freeze over.*

LEFT: *This loon chick, swimming alongside its parent, is in the middle of molting. The molted feathers often float on the water's surface, attracting predators to the presence of young helpless loons. Often less than 10 percent of chicks survive the first three months of life.*

ABOVE: *Young loons can be roughly aged by size and shape. Common loons less than 10 days old look like fluffy tennis balls. By three weeks, they are the size of an elongated grapefruit, and by six weeks the size of a football. At the age of 10 weeks, a juvenile loon is almost equal to an adult in size and shape.*

LEFT: *Loons in the breeding season aggressively chase away other waterfowl, such as these ducks. One way to distinguish juvenile ducks and geese from juvenile loons is by the bills. Ducks and geese have rounded bills; loons have sharp pointed bills.*

ABOVE: *Most loons lay two eggs, or occasionally three. Usually the chicks hatch a day or two apart. The larger sometimes kills its younger sibling, especially in times of limited food. Biologists refer to this as the Cain and Abel syndrome.*

ABOVE: *Common loon chicks may hatch as early as April in the northeastern United States. Red-throated loon chicks in the high Arctic may not hatch until July.*

LEFT: *The long thin neck of the red-throated loon provides excellent camouflage in pondside reeds. A number of predators, including eagles, northern pike, and muskellunge, prey on loons.*

LEFT: *This lone loon sits patiently during an early snowfall, awaiting the mysterious cue that begins the fall migration. It may be the length of the day, the temperature, the barometric pressure or some other factor that humans have yet to fathom that sends many bird species south for the winter.*

ABOVE: *The yellow-billed loon is the loner of the loon family. The largest group of yellow-billed loons ever observed in British Columbia consisted of seven individuals.*

RIGHT: *Some early peoples believed that loon chicks popped out of holes under the female's wings. One 1674 account from the Faeroe Islands states that "the bird has two holes, one under each of its wings, capable to hold an egg."*

In times of rising water levels, loons may continually add to the nest until it towers over 30 centimetres (a foot) high. Such high nests are difficult to enter and leave when the water recedes, however, and many are abandoned.

RIGHT: *This common loon pair probably has a second chick hidden behind one parent. In a recent survey of common loons in Ontario, 71 percent had two chicks.*

LEFT: *Young loons gain weight rapidly on a protein-rich diet that is primarily made up of fish. From a birth weight of only about 85 grams (3 ounces), a common loon grows to about 3.5 kilograms (8 pounds) in only three months.*

ABOVE: *The small, narrow wings of the loon make it a rapid flyer, easily traveling at 98 kilometres (60 miles) an hour, with about 250 to 750 wingbeats a minute. Loons have been reported flying at heights of up to 2057 metres (6748 feet).*

The Pacific loon is probably the most gregarious of the five loon species. Along the western coast of North America, where abundant food is available, large groups of up to 500 Pacific loons have been observed.

RIGHT: *According to an Anishinabeg legend, the first step in the creation of the world was the voice of the Creator calling across the new world; this became the cry of the loon. The second step was the rising of the sun from the blackness; its first beams created splashes of light and dark that became the dappled plumage of the loon.*

THE LOVE OF LOONS

BEYOND THE CALL OF THE WILD

Down the road from my remote country acreage is a small craft shop whose contents reflect the loonmania that has swept the country in recent years. You can buy loon T-shirts, coffee mugs, statues, planters, paperweights, posters, plates, prints, paintings, and recordings. If you're using Canadian currency, the loon graces both the back of the $20 bill and the front of the $1 coin. In Minnesota, where the loon is the beloved state bird, a recording of loon sounds called *Voices of the Loon* has outsold recordings by Prince, the state's own homegrown rock star.

Loons were also revered in ages past by native peoples, who admired the birds' superior swimming and diving skills. One early legend common to many northern native peoples bestows the loon with the exalted title of Earth-Maker. In the beginning, as the legend goes, all the world was water. But the Creator realized that something was lacking, so the

PREVIOUS PAGE, LEFT: *In the 1970s and 1980s, biologists discovered just how badly human activities had harmed the wild world. In 1984, the U.S. Federal Office of Technology Assessment estimated that over 3000 lakes and 37 000 kilometres (23 000 miles) of streams in the U.S. showed high levels of acidity due to acid rain.*

PREVIOUS PAGE, RIGHT: *According to one estimate, there are between 250 000 and 500 000 common loons in Canada. The Ontario common loon population is estimated at about 95 000 breeding birds.*

loon was created to add land to the picture. The loon descended from the heavens, soaring downward until its great speed allowed it to dive deeply into the water. It dove until it reached bottom and then returned to the surface with a bit of mud in its beak. The bit of mud grew and expanded on every side, creating the continents, so from the loon's good deed came forth all of the Earth.

Another legend comes from the Arikara natives of the American plains, who tell the story of Mother Corn leading her people west to a new home. They traveled easily until they were stopped by a great lake. But then a loon appeared and ran across the waters, parting them as Moses parted the Red Sea. The people crossed safely to the other side, and were ever respectful of the loon.

LEFT: *The pristine habitat of the loon is disappearing fast, as lakeside subdivisions, wilderness resorts, and industrial development alter the world of the wild. In Canada, 70 percent of the original wetlands have been destroyed.*

Unfortunately, the loon hasn't always been respected. In the past it has suffered cruel treatment as a source of food, skin, and feathers. Until quite recently, many northern natives made loonskin parkas and hats. Rather than shooting the bird, which would ruin the skin, many loons were snared and then beaten to death.

To the early woodland Cree, loon was a delicacy, but later European arrivals found its dark, fishy-tasting flesh less appealing. In 1766, a Mississippi guide wrote, "It was ill-flavored flesh, but excellent sport." A modern recipe from Maine reflects the bad taste of loon meat: "Skin one loon. Clean it and place it in a large pot with potatoes, turnips, and onions. Salt and pepper to taste. Add one large granite rock about the same weight as the bird. Simmer for five days, adding water as necessary. Remove from heat and cool. Remove the loon. Eat the rock."

Early hunters learned to "toll" a loon, waving a handkerchief or flag to grab the bird's attention and then luring it within bullet range by imitating the bird's call. Even John James Audubon, a name now synonymous with a love of birds, once admitted that tolling was "a form of shooting...which I have often practiced."

In a 1924 account in *Bird Lore* magazine, William Brewster reported, "it was customary to shoot at loons whenever opportunity offered." According to Brewster, "Often the progress of a steamer up the lake was indicated...by the frequent popping of guns fired from decks at Loons and other water-fowl."

During the 1960s there was a growing awareness of the importance of all species to the overall welfare of the world and scientists began recording an alarming decrease in loon

populations. Lakeside developments, recreational lake use, and the thoughtless practice of using waterways as garbage dumps were among the major culprits. In some lakes, loons were forced to swim through a thick layer of flotsam and jetsam: bleach bottles, pop cans, plastic bags, and other miscellaneous broken relics of human existence.

As early as 1795, Samuel Hearne had reported that red-throated loons were "frequently entangled in fishing nets." More recently, entanglement in fishing lines was found to be the second leading cause of loon deaths in New Hampshire. Discarded lead fishing sinkers also took their toll: In one study in New England in the 1970s, 52 percent of loons necropsied had died from lead poisoning. (Loons often ingest small stones to aid digestion, accidentally swallowing lead sinkers in the process.) In Canada, it was estimated that an incredible 445 tonnes (490 tons) worth of lead sinkers were lost in lakes and rivers each year.

Surveys in the 1960s and 1970s revealed that many lakes were devoid of loons. New Hampshire's loon population was down by 75 percent, the bird was rare in Vermont, and it was gone completely from Massachusetts, Connecticut, and Pennsylvania. Even in Alaska, the last refuge for many wild species, it was found that half the population of red-throated loons had disappeared.

Shocked by the widespread loss of loons, bands of Loon Lovers and Loon Rangers formed in many lakeshore communities, alerting residents to the location of loon nests and making artificial nesting platforms for the beleaguered birds. Many communities updated their sewage and garbage disposal laws, making the waters drinkable and safe

PREVIOUS PAGE: *Loons inhabit some of the most remote lakes in North America, but this is scant protection against the heavy hand of humans. In Ontario, 72 percent of loons necropsied between 1993 and 1996 died directly due to human activities.*

LEFT: *Human activities continue to harm loon populations across North America. This common loon in winter plumage was found in California, soaked in oil that likely leaked from or was dumped by a passing ship. Coastal pollution and collisions with pleasure boats also kill hundreds of loons each year.*

for swimming again. Some jurisdictions banned lead sinkers and levied fines against careless fishermen who littered shorelines with deadly fishing line. The birds rebounded, and their eerie call began to echo across Massachusetts waters after a hundred years of silence.

Just as the loon's prospects were improving, a new threat appeared: acid rain. In the 1970s, biologists discovered to their horror that emissions from power plants and automobiles were being widely dispersed by rainfall and concentrated in lakes and ponds. The chemical soup that was created increased the acidity of the water, reducing fish populations to the point where many loons simply starved to death.

In addition, it was found that acid rain helps convert inorganic mercury in lake bottom sediments to a highly poisonous organic form. One-sixth of loons examined in one survey of lakes in northern New England and the Great Lakes had internal levels of mercury known to cause reproductive failure in other waterfowl. Another study found that only two or three parts per million of methyl mercury in loon brain tissues caused less frequent nesting and decreased defense of territory.

Some loons have tried to adapt to human activities by nesting on waters behind dams. But these are dangerous spots to call home. One rise in water levels and the nest is aslosh, drowning precious eggs and chicks. One drop and the nest is high and dry, exposed to hungry predators.

Each year a number of loons are run over by boats and jet skis. And some people who fish still deem loons to be competition, and shoot them on sight.

Today, the loon is protected by the Canadian Migratory Birds Convention and the U.S.

Migratory Bird Treaty, and loon populations are stable in many parts of North America. The common loon's highest numbers in Canada are in Ontario; in the United States, in Minnesota, where dozens of lakes echo with its unforgettable call.

Writers have struggled for decades to describe the loon's various calls, dubbing them haunting, laughing, lonely, eerie, maniacal, and just plain crazy. The loon's tremolo has been described as the cry of a person looking desperately for a loved one or lost friend, the cry of a lost child wailing for its mother, and the cry of a wounded animal calling for help. Poet Robert Bly described it as "the cry of someone who owned very little." Writer John McPhee once wrote, "If it were human, it would be the laugh of the deeply insane."

The distinctive call of the loon is the core of many folk tales. In Norway and Sweden, the call is supposed to herald the coming of rain, leading to the bird's nickname of rain goose. Early B.C. natives similarly named the loon Calls-Up-a-Storm. Faeroe Islanders thought the red-throated loon called when it was following a soul to heaven. The Ojibwa thought the call was an omen of death. The Cree believed it to be the cry of a warrior denied entry to heaven.

A number of North American native legends account for the loon's distinctive voice. One story says that Loon and Crow were out fishing together one day, but Loon was having all the luck. Crow grew angry and in a fit of rage cut out Loon's tongue. To this day, the loon cannot speak but can only call out its hurt-filled cry. Another legend, from the Pacific Northwest, tells of a young boy going to a lake that his mother had warned

PREVIOUS PAGE: *The common loon's striking markings make it one of the most easily recognized and best-loved birds in North America. One measure of this popularity is the thousands of Loon Lakes in British Columbia, Ontario, Washington, Maine, Minnesota, Wisconsin, New York, and Vermont.*

LEFT: *Some natives believed that loons call to summon up winds, to enable them to take flight. Although wind is not a requirement, it does make the take-off easier.*

him was haunted. The boy ignored his mother and caught a fat trout, but the fish was a demon in disguise, and as soon as the boy ate the fish, he was turned into a loon. The boy's mother showed no pity, for she had warned him. And to this day the loon cries out to children to always listen to their mothers.

Whatever story you choose to believe, the effect upon hearing a loon's haunting call is always the same: Your skin tingles, you involuntarily shiver, and you stop everything you are doing to listen in awe to the lonely voice of the North.

Naturalist Sigurd Olson accurately described the loon's call as "the sound that more than any other typifies the wilderness." I like to think that the loon is calling out for the preservation of this endangered wilderness—and it is up to us to listen.

LEFT: *In 1996, Environment Canada and the Canadian Wildife Service reported the results of a 15-year study on acid rain. Of over 200 lakes studied, 56 percent had acidity levels that remained unchanged from 1981–1996; in 11 percent of the lakes, levels of acidity had increased.*

LEFT: *Many loons nest on islands, which provide excellent security against terrestrial predators such as skunks, coyotes, and foxes. Since the 1970s, artificial nesting platforms made of small logs have been used to induce loons to nest on lakes where they have been absent for decades.*

RIGHT: *Many loon nests are located right at the water's edge. In one recent survey in British Columbia, 43 percent of common loon nests were on shore, 35 percent were on islands, and 12 percent were on bare ground with no nest materials.*

ABOVE: *This common loon in winter plumage on the Gulf of Mexico is swimming in dangerous waters, as pollution from oil exploration and human habitation around the Gulf has tainted its once pristine waters.*

Loons do not appear to have suffered as badly from the effects of DDT as other birds. Many raptors showed marked decreases in egg thickness and hatching success until DDT was banned in most of North America.

ABOVE: *This common loon is just beginning to molt. In Canada, the common loon can be found from sea level to elevations as high as 2290 metres (7513 feet).*

RIGHT: *As a symbol of the wilderness, the loon is unsurpassed. If left alone, however, it tolerates humans well. In Anchorage, Alaska, both common and Pacific loons live comfortably within the city limits.*

RIGHT: *In south-central Ontario, 25 percent of recent known loon deaths were from lead poisoning due to lead fishing sinkers. Many jurisdictions have banned such sinkers; nontoxic bismuth sinkers are now available from a number of sources.*

ABOVE: *Loons afflicted with mercury poisoning may not be able to fly, become disoriented, lose weight, and may abandon their nests and chicks. It was not until 1969 that Swedish researchers found that acid rain was aiding in the conversion of the normal inorganic mercury found in the environment to a toxic organic form, with dire consequences.*

RIGHT: *Hawks, owls, eagles, and osprey are all major predators of both loon eggs and loon chicks.*

The call of the loon is the core of many superstitions around the world. In Norway, the call is believed to mean that someone will drown. In the Faeroe Islands, a loon call heard during a funeral means that the loon is accompanying the deceased to heaven.

LEFT: *This loon egg has been cracked by a predator. One survey in Minnesota found that loon nests on islands were twice as safe from predators as those on shore.*

ABOVE: *The Kwakwaka'wakw natives of the British Columbia coast held loons in awe, for they belonged to both air and water, traveling freely between both worlds. Other natives believed that loons guided the souls of the dead to a new world, and should be viewed with reverence.*

RIGHT: *The future of the loon is also our future, for its disappearance from many lakes is a warning that we have polluted the water that is the very basis of life on Earth.*

SUGGESTED READING

Crowley, Kate and Mike Link. *Love of Loons.* Stillwater, Minnesota: Voyageur Press, Inc., 1987.

Dennis, Roy. *Loons.* Stillwater, Minnesota: Voyageur Press, Inc., 1993.

Dregni, Michael, ed. *Loons: Song of the Wild.* Stillwater, Minnesota: Voyageur Press, Inc., 1996.

Fair, Jeff. "Last Call?" *Equinox* no. 77(1994): 52–59.

Taylor, Kip. *Loon.* Aranac, New York: self-published, 1988.

Udvardy, Miklos D.F., ed. *The Audubon Society Field Guide to North American Birds.* New York: Alfred A. Knopf, Inc., 1984.

LOON CONSERVATION GROUPS

North American Loon Fund
6 Lily Pond Road, Gilford, New Hampshire 03246
(http://facstaff.uww.edu/wentzl/nalf/analfhomepage.html)

Canadian Lakes Loon Survey, Bird Studies Canada
P.O. Box 160, Port Rowan, Ontario NOE 1MO
(http://www.bsc-eoc.org)

INDEX

Bold entries refer to photographs.

PHOTO CREDITS

Wayne Lynch 6–7, 12, 15, 19, 22, 25, 28–29, 30, 31, 36, 38, 44, 50, 58–59, 62–63, 64, 65, 66–67, 72–73, 76–77, 79, 84, 88, 93, 98, 103

Daniel J. Cox 10, 11, 16, 20, 32, 37, 39, 42, 52, 68, 74–75, 82, 99

Aubrey Lang 26

Robert Lankinen 33, 34–35, 49, 56, 60, 80–81, 83, 94, 104–105

Thomas Kitchin / First Light 40–41

Robert Lankinen / First Light 43, 46, 55, 70–71,

Terry Attard 61, 102

Dr. Bill Mills / Derek Helmricks 69, 106, 107, 108–109, 110

Bill Silliker Jr. 78

Lynn M. Stone 87

Leslie Degner 91

Brian Milne / First Light 96–97

Donald Standfzield / First Light 100–101, 112–113

Tim Christie 111